☞ **W9-AXS-532**

BIBLE ANSWERS

Studies in the Word of God to Light the Christian Pathway

REVIEW AND HERALD® PUBLISHING ASSOCIATION
HAGERSTOWN, MD 21740

Printed in U.S.A.

Printed in U.S.A.
ISBN 978-0-8280-1147-1
ISBN 978-0-8280-1318-5 AA

Contents

How to Understand the Bible

What did Christ say concerning the study of the Scriptures?

"Search the scriptures; for in them ye think ye have eternal life: and they are they which testify of me." John 5:39.

NOTE.—Christ here refers to the Old Testament Scriptures, the "Bible" of His day. However, His statement is equally true of the New Testament. The same is generally true of the term "scriptures" throughout the New Testament.

For what were the Bereans commended?

"These were more noble than those in Thessalonica, in that they received the word with all readiness of mind, and *searched the scriptures daily, whether those things were so."* Acts 17:11.

NOTE.—"If God's Word were studied as it should be," says a modern Bible student, "men would have a breadth of mind, a nobility of character, and a stability of purpose that is rarely seen in these times. But there is but little profit derived from a hasty reading of the Scriptures. One may read the whole Bible through, and yet fail to see its beauty or comprehend its deep and hidden meaning. One passage studied until its significance is clear to the mind, and its relation to the plan of salvation is evident, is of more value than the perusal of many chapters with no definite purpose in view and no positive instruction gained."

By what comparison is it indicated that some portions of God's Word are more difficult to understand than others?

"For when for the time ye ought to be teachers, ye have need that one teach you again which be *the first principles of the oracles of God;* and are become such as have need of *milk,* and not of *strong meat."* Hebrews 5:12.

In what way is this comparison further explained?

"For every one that useth milk is unskilful in the word of righteousness: for he is a *babe.* But strong meat belongeth to them that are of *full age,* even those who by reason of use have their senses exercised to discern both good and evil." Verses 13, 14.

What writings are specifically mentioned as containing some things difficult to understand?

"And account that the longsuffering of our Lord is salvation; even as our beloved brother *Paul* also according to the wisdom given unto him hath written unto you; as also in all *his epistles,* speaking in them of these things; *in which are some things hard to be understood,* which they that are unlearned and unstable wrest, as they do also the other scriptures, unto their own destruction." 2 Peter 3:15, 16.

NOTE.—Some scriptures are too plain to be misunderstood, while the meaning of others cannot so readily be discerned. To obtain a comprehensive knowledge of any Bible truth, scripture must be compared with scripture, and there should be "careful research and prayerful reflection." But all such study will be richly rewarded.

What did Christ say concerning the book of Daniel?

"When ye therefore shall see the abomination of desolation, spoken of by Daniel the prophet, stand in the holy place, (*whoso readeth, let him understand*)." Matthew 24:15.

What other book of the Bible is especially commended for our study?

"Blessed is he that readeth, and they that hear *the words of this prophecy* [the book Revelation], and keep those things which are written therein: for the time is at hand." Revelation 1:3.

What is one purpose for which the Holy Spirit was sent?

"But the Comforter, which is the Holy Ghost, whom the Father will send in my name, *he shall teach you all things, and bring all things to your remembrance, whatsoever I have said unto you.*" John 14:26.

For what spiritual enlightenment should everyone pray?

"*Open thou mine eyes,* that I may behold wondrous things out of thy law." Psalm 119:18.

Upon what conditions is an understanding of divine things promised?

"Yea, *if thou criest after knowledge, and liftest up thy voice for understanding; if thou seekest her as silver, and searchest for her as for hid treasures;* then shalt thou understand the fear of the Lord, and find the knowledge of God." Proverbs 2:3-5.

What is promised him who wills to do God's will?

"If any man will [literally, "desires" or "wills" to] do his will, *he shall know of the doctrine,* whether it be of God, or whether I speak of myself." John 7:17.

NOTE.—It is proper to repeat again and again the eternal truth that if *any* man will search the word of God for light, with a heart fully submitted to do the will of God as it is revealed to him, that man will receive light.

When asked by the rich young man the conditions of eternal life to what did Jesus direct his attention?

"He said unto him, *What is written in the law? how readest thou?*" Luke 10:26.

NOTE.—The Jews of Christ's day called the first five books of the Bible, which were written by Moses, "the law."

What are the Scriptures able to do for one who believes them?

"And that from a child thou hast known the holy scriptures, *which are able to make thee wise unto salvation through faith which is in Christ Jesus.*" 2 Timothy 3:15.

What great blessing did Christ confer upon His disciples after His resurrection?

"Then opened he their understanding, that they might understand the scriptures." Luke 24:45.

How did Christ reprove those who, though familiar with the letter of the Scriptures, failed to understand them?

"Jesus answered and said unto them, *Ye do err, not knowing the scriptures, nor the power of God."* Matthew 22:29.

Whom did Jesus pronounce blessed?

"But he said, Yea, rather, *blessed are they that hear the word of God, and keep it*." Luke 11:28.

The Fall and Redemption of Man

What is sin declared to be?

"Whosoever committeth sin transgresseth also the law: for *sin is the transgression of the law*." 1 John 3:4.

What precedes the manifestation of sin?

"Then when *lust* hath conceived, it bringeth forth sin." James 1:15.

What is the final result, or fruit, of sin?

"And sin, when it is finished, bringeth forth *death*." Same verse. "The wages of sin is *death*." Romans 6:23.

Upon how many of the human race did death pass as the result of Adam's transgression?

"By one man sin entered into the world, and death by sin; and so *death passed upon all men*, for that all have sinned." Romans 5:12. "In Adam *all die*." 1 Corinthians 15:22.

How were the earth itself and its vegetation affected by Adam's sin?

"Cursed is the ground for thy sake; in sorrow shalt thou eat of it all the days of thy life; *thorns also and thistles shall it bring forth to thee."* Genesis 3:17, 18.

What additional curse came as the result of the first murder?

"And the Lord said unto Cain, ... And *now art thou cursed from the earth,* which hath opened her mouth to receive thy brother's blood from thy hand; *when thou tillest the ground, it shall not henceforth yield unto thee her strength."* Genesis 4:9-12.

What terrible judgment came in consequence of continued sin and transgression against God?

"And the Lord said, I will destroy man whom I have created from the face of the earth." "The end of all flesh is come before me; for the earth is filled with violence." "And Noah was six hundred years old when the *flood of waters* was upon the earth." "The same day were *all the fountains of the great deep broken up, and the windows of heaven were opened."* Genesis 6:7, 13; 7:6, 11.

After the Flood, what came in consequence of further apostasy from God?

"And the Lord came down to see the city and the tower, which the children of men builded. And the Lord said, Behold, the people is one, and they have all one language; and this they begin to do: and now nothing will be restrained from them, which they have imagined to do. Go to, let us go down, and there *confound their language, that they may not understand one another's speech.* So the Lord scattered them abroad from thence upon the face of all the earth: and they left off to build the city." Genesis 11:5-8.

Into what condition has sin brought the entire creation?

"For we know that the whole creation *groaneth* and *travaileth in pain together* until now." Romans 8:22.

What explains God's apparent delay in dealing with sin?

"The Lord is not slack concerning his promise, as some men count slackness; but is *longsuffering to us-ward*, not willing that any should perish, but that all should come to repentance." 2 Peter 3:9.

What is God's attitude toward the sinner?

"For *I have no pleasure in the death of him that dieth*, saith the Lord God: wherefore turn yourselves, and live ye." Ezekiel 18:32.

Can man free himself from the dominion of sin?

"Can the Ethiopian change his skin, or the leopard his spots? *then may ye also do good, that are accustomed to do evil.*" Jeremiah 13:23.

What place has the will in determining whether man shall have life?

"And the Spirit and the bride say, Come. And let him that heareth say, Come. And let him that is athirst come. And *whosoever will, let him take the water of life freely.*" Revelation 22:17.

To what extent has Christ suffered for sinners?

"He was *wounded* for our transgressions, he was *bruised* for our iniquities: the *chastisement* of our peace was upon him; and with his *stripes* we are healed." Isaiah 53:5.

For what purpose was Christ manifested?

"And ye know that *he was manifested to take away our sins;* and in him is no sin. . . . He that committeth sin is of the devil; for the devil sinneth from the beginning. For this purpose the Son of God was manifested, *that he might destroy the works of the devil.*" 1 John 3:5-8.

What was one direct purpose of the incarnation of Christ?

"Forasmuch then as the children are partakers of flesh and blood, he also himself likewise took part of the same; *that through death he might destroy him that had the power of death, that is, the devil.*" Hebrews 2:14.

11

What triumphant chorus will mark the end of the reign of sin?

"And every creature which is in heaven, and on the earth, and under the earth, and such as are in the sea, and all that are in them, heard I saying, *Blessing, and honour, and glory, and power, be unto him that sitteth upon the throne, and unto the Lamb for ever and ever.*" Revelation 5:13.

When and by what means will the effects of sin be removed?

"But the day of the Lord will come as a thief in the night; in the which the heavens shall pass away with a great noise, and *the elements shall melt with fervent heat, the earth also and the works that are therein shall be burned up.*" 2 Peter 3:10.

How thoroughly will the effects of sin be removed?

"And God shall *wipe away all tears* from their eyes; and there shall be *no more death, neither sorrow, nor crying, neither shall there be any more pain, for the former things are passed away.*" Revelation 21:4. *"And there shall be no more curse:* but the throne of God and of the Lamb shall be in it [the Holy City]; and his servants shall serve him." Revelation 22:3.

Will sin and its evil results ever appear again?

"There shall be *no more death.*" "And there shall be *no more curse.*" Revelation 21:4; 22:3.

The Love of God

What is God declared to be?

"God is love." 1 John 4:16.

How great is God's love for the world?

"For God so loved the world, that he gave his only be-gotten Son, that whosoever believeth in him should not perish, but have everlasting life." John 3:16.

In what act especially has God's infinite love been manifested?

"In this was manifested the love of God toward us, be-cause that *God sent his only begotten Son into the world, that we might live through him.*" 1 John 4:9.

In what does God delight?

"Who is a God like unto thee, that pardoneth iniquity, and passeth by the transgression of the remnant of his heritage? he retaineth not his anger for ever, because *he delighteth in mercy.*" Micah 7:18.

How are the mercies of Heaven continually manifested to the sons of men?

"It is of the Lord's mercies that we are not consumed, because his compassions fail not. *They are new every morning:* great is thy faithfulness." Lamentations 3:22, 23.

In view of God's great love, what may we confidently expect?

"He that spared not his own Son, but delivered him up for us all, how shall he not with him also freely *give us all things?* Romans 8:32.

Into what relationship to God does His love bring us?

"Behold, what manner of love the Father hath bestowed upon us, that we should be called *the sons of God.*" 1 John 3:1.

As sons of God to what will we submit? How may we know that we are the sons of God?

"For *as many as are led by the Spirit of God,* they are the sons of God. . . . *The Spirit itself beareth witness with our spirit,* that we are the children of God." Romans 8:14-16.

How is the love of God supplied to the believer?

"And hope maketh not ashamed; because the love of God is shed abroad in our hearts *by the Holy Ghost* which is given unto us." Romans 5:5.

When men appreciate God's love, what will they do?

"How excellent is thy lovingkindness, O God! therefore the children of men *put their trust under the shadow of thy wings.*" Psalm 36:7.

In view of God's great love to us, what attitude should we take toward one another?

"Beloved, if God so loved us, *we ought also to love one another.*" 1 John 4:11.

With what measure of love should we serve others?

"Hereby perceive we the love of God, because he laid

14

down his life for us: and *we ought to lay down our lives for the brethren.*" 1 John 3:16.

Upon what ground does God work for sinners' rest?

"But God, who is rich in mercy, *for his great love wherewith he loved us,* even when we were dead in sins, hath quickened us together with Christ, (by grace ye are saved;) and hath raised *us up together, and made us sit together* in heavenly places in Christ Jesus." Ephesians 2:4-6. (See Titus 3:5, 6.)

What is God's love able to do for His children?

"Nevertheless the Lord thy God would not hearken unto Balaam; but the Lord thy God *turned the curse into a blessing* unto thee, because the Lord thy God loved thee." Deuteronomy 23:5.

In what other way is God's love sometimes shown?

"For whom the Lord loveth he *chasteneth,* and *scourgeth* every son whom he receiveth." Hebrews 12:6.

How enduring is God's love for us?

"The Lord hath appeared of old unto me, saying, Yea, *I have loved thee with an everlasting love:* therefore with lovingkindness have I drawn thee." Jeremiah 31:3.

Can anything separate the true child of God from the love of God?

"For I am persuaded, that neither death, nor life, nor angels, nor principalities, nor powers, nor things present, nor things to come, nor height, nor depth, nor any other creature, shall be able to separate us from the love of God, which is in Christ Jesus our Lord." Romans 8:38, 39.

Unto whom will the saints forever ascribe praise?

"*Unto him that loved us, and washed us from our sins* in his own blood, . . . to him be glory and dominion for ever and ever." Revelation 1:5, 6.

Salvation
Only Through Christ

For what purpose did Christ come into the world?

"This is a faithful saying, and worthy of all acceptation, that Christ Jesus came into the world *to save sinners.*" 1 Timothy 1:15.

Why was He to be named "Jesus"?

"Thou shalt call his name Jesus: *for he shall save his people from their sins.*" Matthew 1:21.

Is there salvation through any other?

"Neither is there salvation in any other: for *there is none other name* under heaven given among men, *whereby we must be saved.*" Acts 4:12.

What has Christ been made for us, and for what purpose?

"For he hath made him to be *sin* for us, who knew no sin; *that we might be made the righteousness of God in him.*" 2 Corinthians 5:21.

How dependent are we upon Christ for salvation?

"Without me ye can do nothing." John 15:5.

What three essentials for a Saviour are found in Christ?

Deity. "But unto the Son he saith, Thy throne, *O God,* is for ever and ever." Hebrews 1:8.

Humanity. "When the fulness of the time was come, God sent forth his Son, *made of a woman,* made under the law." Galatians 4:4.

Sinlessness. "*Who did no sin,* neither was guile found in his mouth." 1 Peter 2:22.

How did Christ show from the Scriptures that the promised Saviour of the world must be both human and divine?

"While the Pharisees were gathered together, Jesus asked them, saying, What think ye of Christ? whose son is he? They say unto him, *The son of David.* He saith unto them, *How then doth David in spirit call him Lord,* saying, The Lord said unto my Lord, Sit thou on my right hand, till I make thine enemies thy footstool? *If David then call him Lord, how is he his son?*" Matthew 22:41-45.

NOTE.—Another has aptly put this important truth concerning the union of the human and divine Christ thus: "Divinity needed humanity that humanity might afford a channel of communication between God and man. Man needs a power out of and above himself to restore him to the likeness of God. There must be a power working from within, a new life from above, before men can be changed from sin to holiness. That power is Christ."

What two facts testify to the union of divinity and humanity in Christ?

"Concerning his Son Jesus Christ our Lord, which was *made of the seed of David according to the flesh; and declared to be the Son of God with power, according to the spirit of holiness, by the resurrection from the dead.*" Romans 1:3, 4.

How complete is the salvation obtained in Christ?

"Wherefore *he is able also to save them to the utter-*

most that come unto God by him, seeing he ever liveth to make intercession for them." Hebrews 7:25.

What should we say for such a Saviour?

"Thanks be unto God for his unspeakable gift." 2 Corinthians 9:15.

Conversion, or the New Birth

How did Jesus emphasize the necessity of conversion?

"Verily I say unto you, *Except ye be converted,* and become as little children, *ye shall not enter into the kingdom of heaven."* Matthew 18:3.

In what other statement did He teach the same truth?

"Verily, verily, I say unto thee, *Except a man be born again,* he cannot see the kingdom of God." John 3:3.

How did He further explain the new birth?

"Jesus answered, Verily, verily, I say unto thee, *Except a man be born of water and of the Spirit,* he cannot enter into the kingdom of God." Verse 5.

With what comparison did He illustrate the subject?

"*The wind* bloweth where it listeth, and thou hearest the sound thereof, but canst not tell whence it cometh, and whither it goeth: *so is every one that is born of the Spirit."* Verse 8.

What takes place when one is converted to Christ?

"Wherefore if any man is in Christ, *he is a new creation:* the old things are passed away; behold, they are become new." 2 Corinthians 5:17, R.V., margin. (See Acts 9:1-22; 22:1-21; 26:1-23.)

Through what was the original creation wrought?

"By the word of the Lord were the heavens made; and all the host of them by the breath of his mouth." Psalm 33:6.

Through what instrumentality is conversion wrought?

"Being born again, not of corruptible seed, but of incorruptible, *by the word of God,* which liveth and abideth for ever." 1 Peter 1:23.

What change is wrought in conversion, or the new birth?

"Even when we were dead in sins, hath *quickened* us [made us alive] together with Christ, (by grace ye are saved;)." Ephesians 2:5.

What is one evidence of this change from death to life?

"We know that we have passed from death unto life, because *we love the brethren.* He that loveth not his brother abideth in death." 1 John 3:14.

From what is a converted sinner saved?

"Let him know, that he which converteth the sinner from the error of his way, shall save a soul from *death,* and shall hide a multitude of sins." James 5:20. (See Acts 26:14-18.)

To whom are sinners brought by conversion?

"Create in me a clean heart, O God; and renew a right spirit within me. Cast me not away from thy presence. . . . Then will I teach transgressors thy ways; and sinners shall be *converted unto thee."* Psalm 51:10-13.

In what words to Peter did Jesus indicate the kind of service a converted person should render to his brethren?

"And the Lord said, Simon, Simon, behold, Satan hath desired to have you, that he may sift you as wheat: but I have prayed for thee, that thy faith fail not: and *when thou art converted, strengthen thy brethren.*" Luke 22:31, 32.

What gracious promise does God make to His people?

"*I will heal their backsliding,* I will love them freely: for mine anger is turned away from him." Hosea 14:4.

By what means is this healing accomplished?

"He [Christ] was wounded for our transgressions, he was bruised for our iniquities: the chastisement of our peace was upon him; and *with his stripes we are healed.*" Isaiah 53:5.

What are the evidences that one has been born of God?

"If ye know that he is righteous, ye know that *every one that doeth righteousness is born of him.*" Beloved, let us love one another: for love is of God; and *every one that loveth is born of God,* and knoweth God." 1 John 2:29; 4:7.

What indwelling power keeps such from sinning?

"Whosoever is born of God doth not commit sin; for *his* [God's] *seed remaineth in him:* and he cannot sin, because he is born of God." 1 John 3:9. (See 1 John 5:4; Genesis 39:9.)

What will be the experience of those born of the Spirit?

"There is therefore now *no condemnation* to them which are in Christ Jesus, who walk not after the flesh, but after the Spirit." Romans 8:1.

What is true of everyone who believes in Jesus?

"Whosoever believeth that Jesus is the Christ is *born of God.*" 1 John 5:1.

21

What change is wrought by beholding Jesus?

"But we all, with open face beholding as in a glass the glory of the Lord, are *changed into the same image* from glory to glory even as by the Spirit of the Lord." 2 Corinthians 3:18.

NOTE.—We were slaves to sin. Jesus came down and suffered with us, and for us, and delivered us. As we behold Him in His word, and in prayer and meditation, and serve Him in the person of others, we may be changed more and more into the glory of His likeness; then, if faithful, we shall someday see Him "face to face."

Christian Baptism

What ordinance is closely associated with believing the gospel?

"And he said unto them, Go ye into all the world, and preach the gospel to every creature. He that believeth and is *baptized* shall be saved; but he that believeth not shall be damned." Mark 16:15, 16.

What did the apostle Peter associate with baptism in his instruction on the day of Pentecost?

"Then Peter said unto them, *Repent,* and be baptized every one of you in the name of Jesus Christ for the remission of sins." Acts 2:38.

In reply to his inquiry concerning salvation, what was the Philippian jailer told to do?

"And they said, *Believe on the Lord Jesus Christ,* and thou shalt be saved, and thy house." Acts 16:31.

What followed immediately after the jailer and his family had accepted Christ as their Saviour?

"And he took them [Paul and Silas] the same hour of

the night, and washed their stripes; and was *baptized,* he and all his, straightway." Verse 33.

In connection with Christian baptism, what is washed away?

"And now why tarriest thou? arise, and be baptized, and *wash away thy sins,* calling on the name of the Lord." Acts 22:16. (See Titus 3:5; 1 Peter 3:21.)

By what means are sins washed away?

"Unto him that loved us, and washed us from our sins *in his own blood.*" Revelation 1:5.

Into whose name are believers to be baptized?

"Go ye therefore, and make disciples of all the nations, baptizing them into the name of the *Father* and of the *Son* and of the *Holy Ghost.*" Matthew 28:19, R.V.

When believers are baptized into Christ, whom do they put on?

"For as many of you as have been baptized into Christ have *put on Christ.*" Galatians 3:27.

Into what experience are those baptized who are baptized into Christ?

"Know ye not, that so many of us as were baptized into Jesus Christ were *baptized into his death?*" Romans 6:3.

NOTE.—Baptism is a gospel ordinance commemorating the *death, burial,* and *resurrection* of Christ. In baptism public testimony is given to the effect that the one baptized has been crucified with Christ, buried with Him, and is raised with Him to walk in newness of life. Only one mode of baptism can rightly represent these facts of experience, and that is immersion—the mode followed by Christ and the primitive church.

How is such a baptism described?

"Therefore we are *buried with him* by baptism into death: that like as Christ was raised up from the dead by the glory of the Father, even so we also should walk in newness of life." Verse 4.

How fully are we thus united with Christ in His experience of death and resurrection?

"For if we have been *planted together* in the likeness of his *death*, we shall be also in the likeness of *his resurrection*." Verse 5.

What will follow this union with Christ in His death and resurrection?

"Now if we be dead with Christ, we believe that we shall also *live with him*." Verse 8.

In what working of God is faith to be exercised in connection with baptism?

"Buried with him in baptism, wherein also ye are risen with him *through the faith of the operation of God, who hath raised him from the dead*." Colossians 2:12.

At the beginning of His ministry, what example did Jesus set for the benefit of His followers?

"Then cometh Jesus from Galilee to Jordan unto John, to be *baptized* of him." Matthew 3:13.

What remarkable experience attended the baptism of Jesus?

"And Jesus, when he was baptized, went up straightway out of the water: and, lo, the heavens were opened unto him, and he saw *the Spirit of God, descending like a dove, and lighting upon him:* and lo a voice from heaven, saying, *This is my beloved Son, in whom I am well pleased*." Verses 16, 17.

What promise is made to those who repent and are baptized?

"Then Peter said unto them, Repent, and be baptized every one of you in the name of Jesus Christ for the remission of sins, and *ye shall receive the gift of the Holy Ghost*." Acts 2:38.

What instruction did the apostle Peter give concerning the Gentiles who had believed?

"Can any man forbid water, that these should not be

baptized, which have received the Holy Ghost as well as we? *And he commanded them to be baptized in the name of the Lord.*" Acts 10:47, 48.

What question did the eunuch ask after Philip had preached Jesus unto him?

"And as they went on their way, they came unto a certain water: and the eunuch said, See, here is water; *what doth hinder me to be baptized?*" Acts 8:36.

In order to baptize the eunuch, where did Philip take him?

"And he commanded the chariot to stand still: and *they went down both into the water,* both Philip and the eunuch; and he baptized him." Verse 38.

How did the people of Samaria publicly testify to their faith in the preaching of Philip?

"But when they believed Philip preaching the things concerning the kingdom of God, and the name of Jesus Christ, *they were baptized,* both men and women." Verse 12.

How perfect is the unity into which believers are brought by being baptized into Christ?

"For as the body is one, and hath many members, and all the members of that one body, being many, are one body: so also is Christ. For by one Spirit are we all *baptized into one body,* whether we be Jews or Gentiles, whether we be bond or free; and have been all *made to drink into one Spirit.*" 1 Corinthians 12:12, 13.

After being united with Christ in the likeness of His death and resurrection, what should the believer do?

"If ye then be risen with Christ, *seek those things which are above,* where Christ sitteth on the right hand of God." Colossians 3:1.

The Law of God

How did God proclaim His law to His people?

"And the Lord spake unto you out of the midst of the fire: ye heard the voice of the words, but saw no similitude; only ye heard a voice. And *he declared unto you his covenant, which he commanded you to perform, even ten commandments; and he wrote them upon two tables of stone.*" Deuteronomy 4:12, 13. (See also Nehemiah 9:13, 14. For the Ten Commandments see Exodus 20:2-17.)

What is the nature of God's law?

"Wherefore the law is *holy,* and the commandment *holy,* and *just,* and *good.*" "For we know that *the law is spiritual:* but I am carnal, sold under sin." Romans 7:12, 14.

NOTE.—In His comments on the sixth and seventh commandments (Matthew 5:21-28) Christ demonstrated the spiritual nature of the law, showing that it relates not merely to outward actions, but also to the thoughts and intents of the heart. (See Hebrews 4:12.) The tenth commandment

27

forbids lust, or all unlawful desire. (Romans 7:7.) Obedience to this law, therefore, requires not merely an outward compliance but genuine heart service. This can be rendered only by a regenerated soul.

"The law of the Lord is perfect, converting the soul." Psalm 19:7. "Is there such a thing as a perfect law? Everything that comes from God is perfect. The law of which we are thinking came from Him. It becomes sullied in our hands. We take from it and try to add to it, and in that way it becomes less than perfect. In a very real sense the law of God is the manifestation of the nature of the Lord. It could no more be imperfect than He is."—*The Augsburg Sunday School Teacher* (Lutheran), August, 1937, vol. 63, no. 8, p. 483, on the Sunday school lesson for August 15.

How comprehensive are these commandments?

"Fear God, and keep his commandments: for *this is the whole duty of man.*" Ecclesiastes 12:13.

Note.—"No human lawgiver could have given forth such a law as that which we find in the decalogue. It is a perfect law; for all human laws that are right are to be found in that brief compendium and epitome of all that is good and excellent toward God, or between man and man."—C. H. Spurgeon, *Sermons*, series 2 (1857), p. 280.

What is the essential principle of the law of God?

"Love worketh no ill to his neighbour: therefore *love* is the fulfilling of the law." Romans 13:10.

What two commandments sum up the law of God?

"Thou shalt love the Lord thy God with all thy heart, and with all thy soul, and with all thy mind. This is the first and great commandment. And the second is like unto it, Thou shalt love thy neighbour as thyself. On these two commandments hang all the law and the prophets." Matthew 22:37-40.

Note.—If you love God with all your heart, you will keep the first table; if you love your neighbor as yourself, you will keep the second.

Why should we fear God and keep His commandments?

"Fear God, and keep his commandments: for this is the

whole duty of man. *For God shall bring every work into judgment,* with every secret thing, whether it be good, or whether it be evil." Ecclesiastes 12:13, 14.

What will be the standard in the judgment?

"So speak ye, and so do, as they that shall be *judged by the law of liberty.*" James 2:12.

What is sin declared to be?

"Whosoever committeth sin transgresseth also the law: for *sin is the transgression of the law.*" 1 John 3:4.

How many of the commandments is it necessary to break in order to become a transgressor of the law?

"For *whosoever shall keep the whole law, and yet offend in one point, he is guilty of all.* For he that said, Do not commit adultery, said also, Do not kill. Now if thou commit no adultery, yet if thou kill, thou art become a transgressor of the law." James 2:10, 11.

NOTE.—"The ten commandments are not ten different laws; they are one law. If I am being held up in the air by a chain with ten links and I break one of them down I come, just as surely as if I break the whole ten. If I am forbidden to go out of an enclosure, it makes no difference at what point I break through."—D. L. MOODY, *Weighed and Wanting* (1898 ed.), p. 119.

"The ten words of Sinai were not ten separate commandments," said G. Campbell Morgan, "but ten sides of the one law of God."—*The Ten Commandments* (Revell, 1901 ed.), p. 11.

"As he [a Methodist] loves God, so he keeps his commandments; not only some, or most of them, but all, from the least to the greatest. He is not content to 'keep the whole law, and offend in one point,' but has, in all points, 'a conscience void of offence towards God and towards man.' "—JOHN WESLEY, *The Character of a Methodist,* in *Works,* vol. 8 (1830 ed.), p. 344.

For what did Christ reprove the Pharisees?

" 'Why do you, too,' He retorted, 'transgress God's commands for the sake of your tradition? God said,

29

"Honour thy father and thy mother" (Exod. xx. 12); and "Let him who reviles father or mother be put to death" (Exod. xxi. 17); but you say: "If a man says to his father or mother, 'This thing is consecrated, otherwise you should have received it from me,' he shall be absolved from honouring his father"; and so you have rendered futile God's word for the sake of your tradition.' " Matthew 15:3-6, Weymouth.

Consequently, how did Christ value their worship?

"But *in vain they do worship me,* teaching for doctrines the commandments of men." Verse 9, A.V.

Can one know God and not keep His commandments?

"He that saith, I know him, and keepeth not his commandments, is *a liar,* and *the truth is not in him.*" 1 John 2:4.

What was Christ's attitude toward God's will, or law?

"Then said I, Lo, I come: in the volume of the book it is written of me, *I delight to do thy will, O my God: yea, thy law is within my heart.*" Psalm 40:7, 8. (See Hebrews 10:5, 7.)

Who did He say would enter the kingdom of heaven?

"Not every one that saith unto me, Lord, Lord, shall enter into the kingdom of heaven; but *he that doeth the will of my Father which is in heaven.*" Matthew 7:21.

How will men be rated in relation to God's commandments?

"Whosoever therefore shall break one of these least commandments, and shall teach men so, *he shall be called the least in the kingdom of heaven:* but *whosoever shall do and teach them,* the same shall be called great in the kingdom of heaven." Matthew 5:19.

NOTE.—"The Ten Commandments constitute a summary of the duties God requires of men. These commandments are the foundation which lies beneath the ethical life of humanity. They are as binding upon Christians today as they were upon the Hebrews who first received them."—*The Snowden-Douglass Sunday School Lessons* for 1946, p. 17. Copyright, 1945, by The Macmillan Company and used by permission.

Why is the carnal mind enmity against God?

"The carnal mind is enmity against God: *for it is not subject to the law of God, neither indeed can be.*" Romans 8:7.

Can man of himself, unaided by Christ, keep the law?

"I am the vine, ye are the branches: he that abideth in me, and I in him, the same bringeth forth much fruit: for *without me ye can do nothing.*" John 15:5. (See Romans 7:14-19.)

What provision has been made by which we are enabled to keep God's law?

"For what the law could not do, in that it was weak through the flesh, God sending his own Son in the likeness of sinful flesh, and for sin, condemned sin in the flesh: that the righteousness of the law might be fulfilled in us, who walk not after the flesh, but after the Spirit." Romans 8:3, 4.

How does the renewed heart regard God's law?

"For this is the love of God, that we keep his commandments: and *his commandments are not grievous.*" 1 John 5:3.

What blessing attends those who keep God's commandments?

"Moreover by them is thy servant warned: and *in keeping of them there is great reward.*" Psalm 19:11.

What would obedience have ensured to ancient Israel?

"O that thou hadst hearkened to my commandments! *then had thy peace been as a river, and thy righteousness as the waves of the sea.*" Isaiah 48:18.

What other blessing attends commandment keeping?

"The fear of the Lord is the beginning of wisdom: *a*

31

good understanding have all they that do his commandments." Psalm 111:10.

What promise is made to the willing and obedient?

"If ye be willing and obedient, *ye shall eat the good of the land.*" Isaiah 1:19.

Penalty
for Transgression

What is the wages of sin?

"The wages of sin is *death*." Romans 6:23. "In the day that thou eatest thereof *thou shalt surely die*." Genesis 2:17. "The soul that sinneth, *it shall die*." Ezekiel 18:4.

How did death enter the world?

"Wherefore, as by one man sin entered into the world, and *death by sin;* and so death passed upon all men, for that all have sinned." Romans 5:12.

God is merciful, but does this clear the guilty?

"The Lord is longsuffering, and of great mercy, forgiving iniquity and transgression, and *by no means clearing the guilty*." Numbers 14:18. (See Exodus 34:5-7.)

What is the result of willful sin?

"*If we sin wilfully* after that we have received the knowledge of the truth, *there remaineth no more sacrifice for sins,* but a certain fearful looking for of judgment and fiery indignation, which shall devour the adversaries. He

33

that despised Moses' law *died without mercy* under two or three witnesses. *Of how much sorer punishment,* suppose ye, *shall he be thought worthy, who hath trodden under foot the Son of God,* and hath counted the blood of the covenant, wherewith he was sanctified, an unholy thing, and hath done despite unto the Spirit of grace?" Hebrews 10:26-29.

To whom has execution of judgment been committed?

"Vengeance is mine; I will repay, saith the Lord." Romans 12:19.

"The Father hath . . . *given to the Son* . . . authority to execute judgment also." John 5:26, 27. (See Jude 14, 15.)

What message has God sent by His ministers?

"Say ye to the righteous, that *it shall be well with him:* for they shall eat the fruit of their doings. *Woe unto the wicked! it shall be ill with him:* for the reward of his hands shall be given him." Isaiah 3:10, 11. *"We are ambassadors for Christ,* as though God did beseech you by us." 2 Corinthians 5:20. (See 2 Timothy 2:24-26.)

To whom is this gift given?

"For God so loved the world, that he gave his only begotten Son, that *whosoever* believeth in him should not perish, but have everlasting life." John 3:16.

How can man escape the penalty of sin?

"The wages of sin is death; but *the gift of God is eternal life through Jesus Christ our Lord."* Romans 6:23.

NOTE.—"God threatens to punish all who transgress these Commandments: we should, therefore, fear his anger, and do nothing against such Commandments. But he promises grace and every blessing to all who keep them: we should, therefore, love and trust in him, and gladly obey his Commandments."—*Luther's Small Catechism* in PHILIP SCHAFF, *The Creeds of Christendom* (Harper), vol. 3, p. 77.

"Through the atonement of Christ more honor is done to the law, and consequently the law is more established, than if the law had been literally executed, and all mankind had been condemned."—JOHNATHAN EDWARDS (Congregationalist), *Works* (1842 ed.), vol. 2, p. 369.

The Resurrection
of the Just

What question does Job ask and answer?

"If a man die, shall he live again? all the days of my appointed time will I wait, till my change come. *Thou shalt call, and I will answer thee:* thou wilt have a desire to the work of thine hands." Job 14:14, 15.

Why did Job wish that his words were written in a book, graven with an iron pen in the rock forever?

"For I know that my redeemer liveth, and that he shall stand at the latter day upon the earth: and though after my skin worms destroy this body, yet *in my flesh shall I see God."* Job 19:25, 26.

When did David say he would be satisfied?

"As for me, I will behold thy face in righteousness: I shall be satisfied, *when I awake, with thy likeness."* Psalm 17:15.

What comforting promise has God made concerning the sleeping saints?

"I will *ransom them from the power of the grave;* I will

redeem them from death: O death, I will be thy plagues; O grave, I will be thy destruction." Hosea 13:14.

Concerning what did Christ tell us not to marvel?

"Marvel not at this: for *the hour is coming, in the which all that are in the graves shall hear his voice, and shall come forth;* they that have done good, unto the resurrection of life; and they that have done evil, unto the resurrection of damnation." John 5:28, 29.

Upon what one fact does Paul base the Christian hope?

"Now if Christ be preached that he rose from the dead, how say some among you that there is no resurrection of the dead? But *if there be no resurrection of the dead, then is Christ not risen: and if Christ be not risen, then is our preaching vain, and your faith is also vain.* Yea, and we are found false witnesses of God; because we have testified of God that *he raised up Christ:* whom he raised not up, if so be that the dead rise not. For *if the dead rise not, then is not Christ raised: and if Christ be not raised, your faith is vain; ye are yet in your sins.* Then they also which are fallen asleep in Christ are *perished.* If in this life only we have hope in Christ, we are of all men most miserable." 1 Corinthians 15:12-19.

What positive declaration does the apostle then make?

"But now is Christ risen from the dead, and become the first-fruits of them that slept. For since by man came death, by man came also the resurrection of the dead. For as in Adam all die, even so in Christ shall all be made alive." Verses 20-22.

NOTE.—The resurrection of Christ is in many respects the most significant fact in history. It is the great and impregnable foundation and hope of the Christian church. Every fundamental truth of Christianity is involved in the resurrection of Christ. If this could be overthrown, every essential doctrine of Christianity would be invalidated. The resurrection of Christ is the pledge of our resurrection and future life.

Concerning what should we not be ignorant?

"But I would not have you to be ignorant, brethren, *concerning them which are asleep,* that ye sorrow not, even as others which have no hope." 1 Thessalonians 4:13.

What is set forth as the basis for hope and comfort?

"For if we believe that Jesus died and rose again, *even so them also which sleep in Jesus will God bring with him.*" Verse 14.

What is said of those embraced in the first resurrection?

"Blessed and holy is he that hath part in the first resurrection: on such the second death hath no power, but they shall be priests of God and of Christ, and shall reign with him a thousand years." Revelation 20:6.

When will this resurrection of the saints take place?

"For this we say unto you by the word of the Lord, that we which are alive and remain unto *the coming of the Lord* shall not prevent [precede] them which are asleep. *For the Lord himself shall descend from heaven* with a shout, with the voice of the archangel, and with the trump of God: *and the dead in Christ shall rise first.*" 1 Thessalonians 4:15, 16.

What will then take place?

"Then we which are alive and remain shall be caught up together with them in the clouds, to meet the Lord in the air: and so shall we ever be with the Lord." Verse 17.

How does Paul say the saints will be raised?

"Behold, I shew you a mystery; We shall not all sleep, but we shall all be changed, in a moment, in the twinkling of an eye, at the last trump: for the trumpet shall sound, and *the dead shall be raised incorruptible.*" 1 Corinthians 15:51, 52.

What great change will then take place in their bodies?

"So also is the resurrection of the dead. It is *sown in corruption;* it is *raised in incorruption:* it is *sown in dishonour;* it is *raised in glory:* it is *sown in weakness;* it is *raised in power:* it is *sown a natural body;* it is *raised a spiritual body.*" Verses 42-44.

What else has He promised to do?

"And God *shall wipe away all tears* from their eyes; and there shall be no more death, neither sorrow, nor crying, neither shall there be any more pain: for the former things are passed away." Revelation 21:4.

A Special Day

When and by whom was the Sabbath made?

"Thus the heavens and the earth were finished, and all the host of them. And *on the seventh day God ended his work* which he had made; *and he rested on the seventh day* from all his work which he had made." Genesis 2:1, 2.

What is the reason for keeping the Sabbath day holy?

"*For in six days the Lord made heaven and earth, the sea, and all that in them is, and rested the seventh day:* wherefore the Lord blessed the sabbath day, and hallowed it." Exodus 20:11.

NOTE.—The Sabbath is the memorial of Creation. God designed that through keeping it man should forever remember Him as the true and living God, the Creator of all things.

Did Christ have anything to do with Creation and the making of the Sabbath?

"All things were made *by him;* and *without him was*

not any thing made that was made." John 1:3. (See also Ephesians 3:9; Colossians 1:16; Hebrews 1:2.)

Note.—Christ was the active agent in Creation. God rested on the seventh day from the work of Creation; therefore, Christ must have rested on the seventh day with the Father. Consequently, it is His rest day as well as the Father's.

After resting on the seventh day, what did God do?

"And God *blessed the seventh day, and sanctified it:* because that in it he had rested from all his work which God created and made." Genesis 2:3.

Note.—By three distinct acts, then, was the Sabbath made: God *rested* on it; He *blessed* it; He *sanctified* it. *Sanctify* means "to make sacred or holy," "to consecrate," "to set apart as sacred."

For whom did Christ say the Sabbath was made?

"And he said unto them, *The sabbath was made for man,* and not man for the sabbath." Mark 2:27.

Note.—*Man* here means "mankind." God instituted the Sabbath to be a source of benefit and blessing to the human family.

"Jesus says: 'The Sabbath was made for man;' and the necessary inference is that from the beginning man knew the primary uses of the day, and received the benefits which it was designed to impart. . . .

"Before the giving of the law from Sinai the obligation of the Sabbath was understood."—J. J. Taylor (Baptist), *The Sabbatic Question* (Revell, 1914 ed.), pp. 20-24.

Regarding the perpetuity of the Sabbath commandment, Moody wrote: "I honestly believe that this commandment is just as binding today as it ever was. I have talked with men who have said that it has been abrogated, but they have never been able to point to any place in the Bible where God repealed it. When Christ was on earth, He did nothing to set it aside; He freed it from the traces under which the scribes and Pharisees had put it, and gave it its true place. 'The sabbath was made for man, not man for the sabbath.' It is just as practicable and as necessary for men to-day as it ever was—in fact, more than ever, because we live in such an intense age.

"The sabbath was binding in Eden, and it has been in force

39

ever since. This fourth commandment begins with the word 'remember' showing that the sabbath already existed when God wrote this law on the tables of stone at Sinai. How can men claim that this one commandment has been done away with when they will admit that the other nine are still binding?"—D. L. Moody, *Weighed and Wanting* (1898 ed.), pp. 46, 47.

When did God bless and sanctify the seventh day?

"And on the seventh day God ended his work which he had made; and he rested on the seventh day from all his work which he had made. And God blessed the seventh day, and sanctified it: *because that in it he* HAD *rested from all his work* which God created and made." Genesis 2:2, 3.

NOTE.—"If we had no other passage than this of Genesis 2:3, there would be no difficulty in deducing from it a precept for the universal observance of a Sabbath, or seventh day, to be devoted to God as holy time, by all of that race for whom the earth and its nature were specially prepared. The first men must have known it. The words 'He hallowed it' can have no meaning otherwise. They would be a blank unless in reference to some who were required to keep it holy."—John Peter Lange, *A Commentary on the Holy Scriptures,* on Genesis 2:3, vol. 1, p. 197.

What does the Sabbath commandment require?

"*Remember the sabbath day, to keep it holy.* Six days shalt thou labour, and do all thy work: but the seventh day is the sabbath of the Lord thy God: *in it thou shalt not do any work*, thou, nor thy son, nor thy daughter, thy manservant, nor thy maidservant, nor thy cattle, nor thy stranger that is within thy gates." Exodus 20:8-10.

NOTE.—Luther says, on Exodus 16:4, 22-30: "Hence you can see that the Sabbath was before the law of Moses came, and has existed from the beginning of the world. Especially have the devout, who have preserved the true faith, met together and called upon God on this day." Translated from *Auslegung des Alten Testaments* (Commentary on the Old Testament), in *Sammtliche Schriften* (Collected Writings), edited by J. G. Walch, vol. 3, col. 950.

How did God prove Israel in the wilderness?

"I will rain bread from heaven for you; and the people shall go out and gather a certain rate every day, *that I may prove them, whether they will walk in my law, or no."* Exodus 16:4.

On which day was a double portion of manna gathered?

"And it came to pass, that *on the sixth day they gathered twice as much bread,* two omers for one man." Verse 22.

What did Moses say to the rulers?

"This is that which the Lord hath said, To morrow is the rest of the holy sabbath unto the Lord." Verse 23.

NOTE.—"2. The Sabbath is indispensable to man, being promotive of his highest good, physically, intellectually, socially, spiritually, and eternally. Hence its observance is connected with the best of promises, and its violation with the severest penalties. Exod. xxiii, 12; xxxi, 12-18; Neh. xiii, 15-22; Isa. lvi, 2-7; lviii, 13-14; Jer. xvii, 21-27; Ezek. xx, 12-13; xxii, 26-31. Its sanctity was very distinctly marked in the gathering of the manna. Exod. xvi, 22-30.

"3. The original law of the Sabbath was renewed and made a prominent part of the moral law, or ten commandments, given through Moses at Sinai. Exod. xx, 8-11."—AMOS BINNEY AND DANIEL STEELE, *Binney's Theological Compend Improved* (1902 ed.), p. 170.

What did some of the people do on the seventh day?

"It came to pass, that *there went out some of the people on the seventh day for to gather,* and they found none." Verse 27.

How did God reprove their disobedience?

"And the Lord said unto Moses, *How long refuse ye to keep my commandments and my laws?"* Verse 28.

Why was twice as much manna given on the sixth day?

"See, *for that the Lord hath given you the sabbath, therefore he giveth you on the sixth day the bread of two days;* abide ye every man in his place, let no man go out of his place on the seventh day." Verse 29.

How, then, did the Lord test the people?

Over the keeping of the Sabbath.

NOTE.—Thus we see that the Sabbath commandment was a part of God's law before this law was spoken from Sinai, for this incident occurred before Israel came to Sinai.

The Change
of the Sabbath

Of what is the Sabbath commandment a part?

The law of God. (See Exodus 20:8-11.)

In His most famous sermon, what did Christ say of the law?

"Think not that I am come to destroy the law, or the prophets: I am not come to destroy, but to fulfil." Matthew 5:17.

NOTE.—"He [Christ] fulfilled the moral law by obeying, by bringing out its fulness of meaning, by showing its intense spirituality, and He established it on a surer basis than ever as the eternal law of righteousness. He fulfilled the ceremonial and typical law, not only by conforming to its requirements, but by realizing its spiritual significance. He filled up the shadowy outlines of the types, and, thus fulfilled, they pass away, and it is no longer necessary for us to observe the Passover or slay the daily lamb; we have the substance in Christ."—*The International Standard Bible Encyclopaedia,* vol. 3, p. 1847.

How enduring did He say the law is?

"Till heaven and earth pass, one jot or one tittle shall in no wise pass from the law, till all be fulfilled." Verse 18.

What did He say of those who should break one of the least of God's commandments, and teach men so to do?

"Whosoever therefore shall break one of these least commandments, and shall teach men so, *he shall be called the least in the kingdom of heaven.*" Verse 19.

Note.—From this it is evident that all ten commandments are binding in the Christian dispensation, and that Christ had no thought of changing any of them. One of these commands the observance of the seventh day as the Sabbath. But most Christians keep the first day of the week instead.

Many believe that Christ changed the Sabbath. But, from His own words, we see that He came for no such purpose. The responsibility for this change must therefore be looked for elsewhere.

What did God, through the prophet Daniel, say the power represented by the "little horn" would think to do?

"He shall speak words against the Most High, and shall wear out the saints of the Most High; and *shall think to change the times and the law.*" Daniel 7:25, R.S.V.

What did the apostle Paul say the "man of sin" would do?

"For that day shall not come, except there come a falling away first, and that man of sin be revealed, the son of perdition; *who opposeth and exalteth himself above all that is called God, or that is worshipped.*" 2 Thessalonians 2:3, 4.

Note.—An effective way by which a power could exalt itself above God would be by assuming to change the law of God, and by requiring obedience to its own law instead of God's law.

What power has claimed authority to change God's law?

The papacy.

Note.—"The pope is of so great authority and power that he can modify, explain, or interpret even divine laws. . . .

44

The pope can modify divine law, since his power is not of man, but of God, and he acts as vicegerent of God upon earth."—Translated from Lucius Ferraris, *Prompta Bibliotheca* (Ready Library), "Papa," art. 2.

What part of the law of God has the papacy thought to change?

The fourth commandment.

Note.—"They [the Catholics] allege the change of the Sabbath into the Lord's day, contrary, as it seemeth, to the Decalogue; and they have no example more in their mouths than the change of the Sabbath. They will needs have the Church's power to be very great, because it hath dispensed with a precept of the Decalogue."—The Augsburg Confession (Lutheran), part 2, art. 7, in Philip Schaff, *The Creeds of Christendom* (Harper), vol. 3, p. 64.

"It [the Roman Catholic Church] *reversed* the Fourth Commandment by doing away with the Sabbath of God's word, and instituting Sunday as a holiday."—N. Summerbell, *History of the Christian Church* (1873), p. 415.

Does the papacy acknowledge changing the Sabbath?

It does.

Note.—The *Catechismus Romanus* was commanded by the Council of Trent and published by the Vatican Press, by order of Pope Pius V, in 1566. This catechism for priests says: "It pleased the church of God, that the religious celebration of the Sabbath day should be transferred to 'the Lord's day.' "—*Catechism of the Council of Trent* (Donovan's translation, 1867), part 3, chap. 4, p. 345. The same in slightly different wording, is in the McHugh and Callan translation (1937 ed.), p. 402.

"*Ques.*—How prove you that the church hath power to command feasts and holydays?

"*Ans.*—By the very act of changing the Sabbath into *Sunday*, which Protestants allow of; and therefore they fondly contradict themselves, by keeping *Sunday* strictly, and breaking most other feasts commanded by the same Church."—Henry Tuberville, *An Abridgment of the Christian Doctrine* (1833 approbation), p. 58. (Same statement in *Manual of Christian Doctrine*, ed. by Daniel Ferris [1916 ed.], p. 67.)

"*Ques.*—Which is the Sabbath day?

"*Ans.*—Saturday is the Sabbath day.

"*Ques.*—Why do we observe Sunday instead of Saturday?

"*Ans.*—We observe Sunday instead of Saturday because the Catholic Church transferred the solemnity from Saturday to Sunday."—PETER GEIERMANN, *The Convert's Catechism of Catholic Doctrine* (1946 ed.), p. 50. Geiermann received the "apostolic blessing" of Pope Pius X on his labors, Jan. 25, 1910.

Do Catholic authorities acknowledge that there is no command in the Bible for the sanctification of Sunday?

They do.

NOTE.—"You may read the Bible from Genesis to Revelation, and you will not find a single line authorizing the sanctification of Sunday. The Scriptures enforce the religious observance of Saturday, a day which we never sanctify."— JAMES CARDINAL GIBBONS, *The Faith of Our Fathers* (1917 ed.), pp. 72, 73.

"Nowhere in the Bible is it stated that worship should be changed from Saturday to Sunday. The fact is that the Church was in existence for several centuries before the Bible was given to the world. The Church made the Bible, the Bible did not make the Church.

"Now the Church . . . instituted, by God's authority, Sunday as the day of worship. This same Church, by the same divine authority, taught the doctrine of Purgatory long before the Bible was made. We have, therefore, the same authority for Purgatory as we have for Sunday."—MARTIN J. SCOTT, *Things Catholics Are Asked About* (1927 ed.), p. 136.

Do Protestant writers acknowledge the same?

They do.

NOTE.—"The Lord's day was merely of ecclesiastical institution. It was not introduced by virtue of the fourth commandment."—JEREMY TAYLOR (Church of England), *Ductor Dubitantium,* part 1, book 2, chap. 2, rule 6, secs. 51, 59 (1850 ed.), vol. 9, pp. 458, 464.

"The Lord's Day is not sanctified by any specific command or by any inevitable inference. In all the New Testament there is no hint or suggestion of a legal obligation binding any man, whether saint or sinner, to observe the Day. Its sanctity arises only out of what it means to the true believer."—J. J. TAYLOR (Baptist), *The Sabbatic Question*, p. 72.

"Because it was requisite to appoint a certain day, that the people might know when they ought to come together, it appears that the [Christian] Church did for that purpose appoint the Lord's day."—Augsburg Confession, part 2, art. 7, in PHILIP SCHAFF, *The Creeds of Christendom* (Harper), vol. 3, p. 69.

"And where are we told in the Scriptures that we are to keep the first day at all? We are commanded to keep the seventh; but we are nowhere commanded to keep the first day. . . . The reasons why we keep the first day of the week holy instead of the seventh is for the same reason that we observe many other things, not because the Bible, but because the church, has enjoined it."—ISAAC WILLIAMS (Anglican), *Plain Sermons on the Catechism*, vol. 1, pp. 334, 336.

How did this change in observance of days come about?

Through a *gradual* transference.

NOTE.—"The Christian Church made no formal, but a *gradual* and almost unconscious, transference of the one day to the other."—F. W. FARRAR, *The Voice From Sinai*, p. 167. This of itself is evidence that there was no divine command for the change of the Sabbath.

For how long a time was the seventh-day Sabbath observed in the Christian church?

For many centuries. In fact, its observance has never wholly ceased in the Christian church.

NOTE.—Mr. Morer, a learned clergyman of the Church of England, says: "The *Primitive Christians* had a great veneration for the *Sabbath*, and spent the *Day* in Devotion and Sermons. And 'tis not to be doubted but they derived this Practice from the *Apostles* themselves."—*A Discourse in Six Dialogues on the Name, Notion, and Observation of the Lord's Day*, p. 189.

"A history of the problem shows that in some places, it was really only after some centuries that the Sabbath rest really was entirely abolished, and by that time the practice of observing a bodily rest on the Sunday had taken its place."—VINCENT J. KELLY, *Forbidden Sunday and Feast-Day Occupations*, p. 15.

Lyman Coleman says: "Down even to the fifth century the observance of the Jewish Sabbath was continued in the Christian church, but with a rigor and a solemnity gradually diminishing until it was wholly discontinued."—*Ancient Christianity Exemplified,* chap. 26, sec. 2.

The church historian Socrates, who wrote in the fifth century, says: "Almost all the churches throughout the world celebrate the sacred mysteries on the Sabbath of every week, yet the Christians of Alexandria and at Rome, on account of some ancient tradition, have ceased to do this."—*Ecclesiastical History,* book 5, chap. 22, in *A Select Library of Nicene and Post-Nicene Fathers,* 2d. series, vol. 2, p. 32.

Sozomen, another historian of the same period, writes: "The people of Constantinople, and almost everywhere, assemble together on the Sabbath, as well as on the first day of the week, which custom is never observed at Rome or at Alexandria."—*Ecclesiastical History,* book 7, chap. 19, in the same volume as the above quotation.

All this would have been inconceivable had there been a divine command given for the change of the Sabbath. The last two quotations also show that Rome led in the apostasy and in the change of the Sabbath.

How did Sunday observance originate?

As a voluntary celebration of the resurrection, a custom without pretense of divine authority.

NOTE.—"Opposition to Judaism introduced the particular festival of Sunday very early, indeed, into the place of the Sabbath. . . . The festival of Sunday, like all other festivals, was always only a human ordinance, and it was far from the intentions of the apostles to establish a Divine command in this respect, far from them, and from the early apostolic Church, to transfer the laws of the Sabbath to Sunday. Perhaps, at the end of the second century a false application of this kind had begun to take place; for men appear by that time to have considered labouring on Sunday as a sin."—AUGUSTUS NEANDER, *The History of the Christian Religion and Church* (Rose's translation from the 1st German ed.), p. 186.

Who first enjoined Sundaykeeping by law?

Constantine the Great.

NOTE.—"The earliest recognition of the observance of Sunday as a legal duty is a constitution of Constantine in 321 A.D., enacting that all courts of justice, inhabitants of towns, and workshops were to be at rest on Sunday (*venerabili die solis*), with an exception in favor of those engaged in agricultural labor."—*Encyclopaedia Britannica*, 11th ed., art. "Sunday."

"On the venerable Day of the Sun let the magistrates and people residing in cities rest, and let all workshops be closed. In the country, however, persons engaged in agriculture may freely and lawfully continue their pursuits; because it often happens that another day is not so suitable for grain-sowing or for vine planting; lest by neglecting the proper moment for such operations the bounty of heaven should be lost. (Given the 7th day of March, Crispus and Constantine being consuls each of them for the second time.)"—*Codex Justinianus*, lib. 3, tit. 12, 3; translated in *History of the Christian Church*, by Philip Schaff (Scribners, 1902 ed.), vol. 3, p. 380.

This edict, issued by Constantine, who first opened the way for the union of church and state in the Roman Empire, in a manner supplied the lack of a divine command for Sunday observance. It was one important step in bringing about and establishing the change of the Sabbath.

What testimony does Eusebius bear on this subject?

"All things whatsoever that it was duty to do on the Sabbath, these *we* [the church] have transferred to the Lord's day."—Translated from EUSEBIUS, *Commentary on the Psalms*, in Migne, *Patrologia Graeca*, vol. 23, cols. 1171, 1172.

NOTE.—The change of the Sabbath was the result of the combined efforts of church and state, and it took centuries to accomplish it. Eusebius of Caesarea (270-338) was a noted bishop of the church, biographer and flatterer of Constantine, and the reputed father of ecclesiastical history.

By what church council was the observance of the seventh day forbidden and Sunday observance enjoined?

The Council of Laodicea, in Asia Minor, fourth century.

NOTE.—Canon 29 reads: "Christians shall not Judaize and be idle on Saturday [*sabbato*, the Sabbath], but shall work on that day; but the Lord's day they shall especially honour, and, as being Christians, shall, if possible, do no work on that day. If, however, they are found Judaizing, they shall be shut out [*anathema*] from Christ."—CHARLES JOSEPH HEFELE, *A History of the Councils of the Church*, vol. 2 (1896 English ed.), p. 316.

What was done at the Council of Laodicea was but one of the steps by which the change of the Sabbath was effected. It was looked back upon as the first church council to forbid Sabbath observance and enjoin Sunday rest as far as possible, but it was not so strict as later decrees. Different writers give conflicting dates for this Council of Laodicea. The exact date is unknown, but may be placed "generally somewhere between the years 343 and 381." (Hefele, vol. 2, p. 298.)

What do Catholics say of Protestant Sundaykeepers?

They are obeying the authority of the Catholic Church.

NOTE.—"For ages all Christian nations looked to the Catholic Church, and, as we have seen, the various states enforced by law her ordinances as to worship and cessation of Labor on Sunday. Protestantism, in discarding the authority of the church, has no good reason for its Sunday theory, and ought logically, to keep Saturday as the Sabbath."

"The State, in passing laws for the due Sanctification of Sunday, is unwittingly acknowledging the authority of the Catholic Church and carrying out more or less faithfully its prescriptions.

"The Sunday, as a day of the week set apart for the obligatory public worship of Almighty God, to be sanctified by a suspension of all servile labor, trade, and worldly avocations and by exercises of devotion, *is purely a creation of the Catholic Church.*"—*The American Catholic Quarterly Review*, January, 1883, pp. 152, 139.

What determines whose servants we are?

"Know ye not, that to whom ye yield yourselves servants to obey, *his servants ye are to whom ye obey?*" Romans 6:16.

When asked to bow to Satan, how did Christ reply?

"It is written, Thou shalt worship the Lord thy God, and *him only shalt thou serve.*" Matthew 4:10.

What kind of worship does the Saviour call that which is not according to God's commandments?

"But *in vain they do worship me, teaching for doctrine the commandments of men.*" Matthew 15:9.

What appeal did Elijah make to apostate Israel?

"How long halt ye between two opinions? *if the Lord be God, follow him: but if Baal, then follow him.*" 1 Kings 18:21.

NOTE.—In times of ignorance God winks at that which otherwise would be sin; but when light comes He commands men everywhere to repent. (Acts 17:30.) The period during which the saints, times, and the law of God were to be in the hands of the papacy has expired (Daniel 7:25); the true light on the Sabbath question is now shining; and God is sending a message to the world, calling upon men to fear and worship Him, and to return to the observance of His holy rest day, the seventh-day Sabbath. (Revelation 14:6-12.)

Nebuchadnezzar's Dream

What statement did Nebuchadnezzar, king of Babylon, make to his wise men whom he had assembled?

"And the king said unto them, *I have dreamed a dream, and my spirit was troubled to know the dream.*" Daniel 2:3.

After the wise men had thus confessed their inability to do what the king required, who offered to interpret the dream?

"Then *Daniel* went in, and desired of the king that he would give him time, and that he would shew the king the interpretation." Verse 16.

What did Daniel say the king had seen in his dream?

"Thy dream, and the visions of thy head upon thy bed, are these; . . . Thou, O king, sawest, and behold *a great image*. This great image, whose brightness was excellent, stood before thee; and the form thereof was terrible." Verses 28-31.

Of what were the different parts of the image composed?

"This image's head was of fine *gold,* his breast and his

arms of *silver,* his belly and his thighs of *brass,* his legs of *iron,* his feet *part of iron and part of clay."* Verses 32, 33.

By what means was the image broken to pieces?

"Thou sawest till that *a stone* was cut out without hands, which smote the image upon his feet that were of iron and clay, and brake them to pieces." Verse 34.

What became of the various parts of the image?

"Then was the iron, the clay, the brass, the silver, and the gold, broken to pieces together, and *became like the chaff of the summer threshingfloors; and the wind carried them away,* that no place was found for them: and the stone that smote the image became a great mountain, and filled the whole earth." Verse 35.

With what words did Daniel begin the interpretation of the dream?

"Thou, O king, art a king of kings: for the God of heaven hath given thee a kingdom, power, and strength, and glory. And wheresoever the children of men dwell, the beasts of the field and the fowls of the heaven hath he given into thine hand, and hath made thee ruler over them all. *Thou art this head of gold."* Verses 37, 38.

NOTE.—The character of the Neo-Babylonian Empire is fittingly indicated by the nature of the material composing that portion of the image by which it was symbolized—the head of gold. It was "the golden kingdom of a golden age." The metropolis, Babylon, reached a height of unrivaled magnificence.

What was to be the nature of the next kingdom?

"After thee shall arise another kingdom *inferior to thee."* Verse 39, first part.

Who was the last Babylonian king?

"In that night was *Belshazzar* the king of the Chaldeans slain. And Darius the Median took the kingdom, being about threescore and two years old." Daniel 5:30, 31.

To whom was Belshazzar's kingdom given?

"Thy kingdom is divided, and given to *the Medes and Persians.*" Verse 28.

By what is this kingdom of the Medes and Persians— the Persian Empire—represented in the great image?

The breast and arms of silver. (Daniel 2:32.)

By what is the Greek, or Macedonian, Empire, which succeeded the kingdom of the Medes and Persians, represented in the image?

"His belly and his thighs of *brass.*" Verse 32. "And another *third kingdom of brass,* which shall bear rule over all the earth." Verse 39.

NOTE.—That the empire which replaced the Persian was the Greek is clearly stated in Daniel 8:5-8, 20, 21. The Greco-Macedonian Empire existed in two stages, first united under Alexander the Great and then divided under his successors.

What is said of the fourth kingdom?

"And the fourth kingdom *shall be strong as iron:* forasmuch as iron breaketh in pieces and subdueth all things: and as iron that breaketh all these, *shall it break in pieces and bruise.*" Verse 40.

NOTE.—It is well known that the great world power that absorbed the fragments of the empire of Alexander the Great was Rome.

What was indicated by the mixture of clay and iron in the feet and toes of the image?

"And whereas thou sawest the feet and toes, part of potters' clay, and part of iron, *the kingdom shall be divided.*" Verse 41.

NOTE.—The barbarian tribes that overran the Roman Empire formed the kingdoms which developed into the nations of modern Europe.

In what prophetic language was the varying strength of the ten kingdoms of the divided empire indicated?

"And as the toes of the feet were *part of iron, and part*

of clay, so the kingdom shall be *partly strong, and partly broken* [literally, *"brittle"*]." Verse 42.

Were any efforts to be made to reunite the divided empire of Rome?

"And whereas thou sawest iron mixed with miry clay, *they shall mingle themselves with the seed of men:* but they shall not cleave one to another, even as iron is not mixed with clay." Verse 43.

NOTE.—Charlemagne, Charles V, Louis XIV, Napoleon, Kaiser Wilhelm, and Hitler all tried to reunite the broken fragments of the Roman Empire and failed. By marriage and intermarriage of royalty ties have been formed with a view to strengthening and cementing together the shattered kingdom, but none have succeeded. The element of disunion remains. Many political revolutions and territorial changes have occurred in Europe since the end of the Western Roman Empire in A.D. 476; but its divided state still remains.

This remarkable dream, as interpreted by Daniel, represents in the briefest form, and yet with unmistakable clearness, a series of world empires from the time of Nebuchadnezzar to the close of earthly history and the setting up of the everlasting kingdom of God. History confirms the prophecy.

What is to take place in the days of these kingdoms?

"And in the days of these kings shall *the God of heaven set up a kingdom, which shall never be destroyed:* ... *but it shall break in pieces and consume all these kingdoms, and it shall stand for ever." Verse 44.*

NOTE.—This verse foretells the establishment of another universal kingdom, the kingdom of God. This kingdom is to overthrow and supplant all existing earthly kingdoms, and is to stand forever. The time for the setting up of this kingdom was to be "in the days of these kings." This cannot refer to the four preceding empires, or kingdoms, for they were not contemporaneous, but successive; neither can it refer to an establishment of the kingdom at Christ's first advent, for the ten kingdoms which arose out of the ruins of the Roman Empire were not yet in existence. It must therefore refer to the divided kingdoms, or nations, that succeeded Rome, represented by the present nations of Europe. This final kingdom, then, is yet future.

In what announcement in the New Testament is the establishment of the kingdom of God made known?

"And the seventh angel sounded; and there were great voices in heaven, saying, *The kingdoms of this world are become the kingdoms of our Lord, and of his Christ;* and he shall reign for ever and ever." Revelation 11:15.

Our Lord's
Great Prophecy

How did Christ feel concerning Jerusalem?

"And when he was come near, he beheld the city, and *wept over it,* saying, If thou hadst known, even thou, at least in this thy day, the things which belong unto thy peace! but now they are hid from thine eyes." Luke 19:41, 42.

In what words did He foretell its destruction?

"Thine enemies shall cast a trench about thee, and compass thee round, and keep thee in on every side, and shall lay thee even with the ground, and thy children within thee; and they shall not leave in thee one stone upon another; because thou knewest not the time of thy visitation." Verses 43, 44.

What pitiful appeal did He make to the impenitent city?

"O Jerusalem, Jerusalem, thou that killest the prophets, and stonest them which are sent unto thee, how often would I have gathered thy children together, even as a

57

hen gathereth her chickens under her wings, and ye would not!" Matthew 23:37.

As He was about to leave the Temple, what did He say?

"Behold, your house is left unto you *desolate*." Verse 38.

NOTE.—The Jews filled up their cup of iniquity by their final rejection and crucifixion of Christ, and their persecution of His followers after His resurrection. (See Matthew 23:29-35; John 19:15; Acts 4 to 8.)

Hearing these words, what questions did the disciples ask?

"Tell us, when shall these things be? and what shall be the sign of thy coming, and of the end of the world?" Matthew 24:3.

NOTE.—The overthrow of Jerusalem and of the Jewish nation is a type of the final destruction of all the cities of the world, and of all nations. The descriptions of the two events seem to be blended. Christ's prophetic words reached beyond Jerusalem's destruction to the final conflagration; they were spoken not for the early disciples only but also for those who were to live during the closing scenes of the world's history. Christ gave definite signs, both of the destruction of Jerusalem and of His second coming.

Did Christ indicate that either event was imminent?

"Jesus answered and said unto them, *Take heed that no man deceive you.* For many shall come in my name, saying, I am Christ; and shall deceive many. And ye shall hear of wars and rumours of wars: see that ye be not troubled: *for all these things must come to pass, but the end is not yet*." Verses 4-6.

What did He say of the wars, famines, pestilences, and earthquakes that were to precede these events?

"All these are *the beginning of sorrows*." Verse 8.

NOTE.—These were to precede and culminate in the overthrow, first, of Jerusalem, and finally, of the whole world; for, as already noted, the prophecy has a double application, first, to Jerusalem and the Jewish nation, and second, to the

58

whole world. The destruction of Jerusalem for its rejection of Christ at His first coming was a type of the destruction of the world at the end for its rejection of Christ in refusing to heed the closing warning message sent by God to prepare the world for Christ's second advent.

What would be the experiences of His people?

"Then shall they deliver you up to be afflicted, and shall kill you: and ye shall be hated of all nations for my name's sake. And then shall many be offended, and shall betray one another, and shall hate one another. And many false prophets shall rise, and shall deceive many. And because iniquity shall abound, the love of many shall wax cold." Verses 9-12.

Who did He say would be saved?

"But *he that shall endure unto the end,* the same shall be saved." Verse 13.

When did Christ say the end would come?

"And *this gospel of the kingdom* shall be *preached in all the world* for a *witness* unto *all nations;* and *then shall the end come."* Verse 14.

NOTE.—Before the fall of Jerusalem, Paul carried the gospel to Rome—then the capital of the world. He wrote of the saints of "Caesar's household" (Philippians 4:22), and further said that the gospel had been "preached to every creature which is under heaven." Colossians 1:23.

Thus it was respecting the end of the Jewish nation; and thus it will be in the end of the world as a whole. When the gospel, or good news, of Christ's coming kingdom has been preached in all the world for a witness unto all nations, then the end will come. As the end of the Jewish nation came with overwhelming destruction, so will come the end of the world.

What would be a sign of the fall of Jerusalem?

"And *when ye shall see Jerusalem compassed with armies,* then know that the desolation thereof is nigh." Luke 21:20.

When the sign appeared, what were the disciples to do?

"When ye therefore shall see the abomination of desolation, spoken of by Daniel the prophet, stand in the holy place, (whoso readeth, let him understand:) then let them which be in Judaea *flee into the mountains.*" Matthew 24:15, 16.

NOTE.—In A.D. 66, when Cestius came against the city, but unaccountably withdrew, the Christians discerned in this the sign foretold by Christ, and fled (Eusebius, *Church History,* book 3, chap. 5), while 1,100,000 Jews are said to have been killed in the terrible siege in A.D. 70. Here is a striking lesson on the importance of studying the prophecies and heeding the signs of the times. Those who believed Christ and watched for the sign which He had foretold were saved, while the unbelieving perished. So in the end of the world the watchful and believing will be delivered, while the careless and unbelieving will be snared and taken. (See Matthew 24:36-44; Luke 21:34-36; 1 Thessalonians 5:1-6.)

When the sign appeared, how suddenly were they to flee?

"Let him which is on the housetop not come down to take any thing out of his house: neither let him which is the field return back to take his clothes." Verses 17, 18.

How did Christ further show His care for His disciples?

"But pray ye that your flight be not in *the winter,* neither on *the sabbath day.*" Verse 20.

NOTE.—Flight in winter would entail discomfort and hardship; an attempt to flee on the Sabbath would doubtless meet with difficulty.

The prayers of Christ's followers were heard. Events were so overruled that neither Jews nor Romans hindered their flight. When Cestius retreated, the Jews pursued his army, and the Christians thus had an opportunity to leave the city. The country was cleared of enemies, for at the time of this siege, the Jews had assembled at Jerusalem for the Feast of Tabernacles. Thus the Christians of Judea were able to escape unmolested, and in the autumn, a most favorable time for flight.

What trying experience did Christ then foretell?

"For *then shall be great tribulation,* such as was not since the beginning of the world to this time, no, nor ever shall be." Verse 21.

NOTE.—In the siege of Jerusalem a prophecy of Moses (Deuteronomy 28:47-53) was literally fulfilled: "Thou shalt eat the fruit of thine own body, the flesh of thy sons and of thy daughters, ... in the siege, and in the straitness, wherewith thine enemies shall distress thee." For the fulfillment, see Josephus, *Wars of the Jews,* book 6, chap. 3, par. 4.

Following the destruction of Jerusalem came the persecution of the Christians under pagan emperors during the first three centuries of the Christian Era. Later came the greater and more terrible persecution during the long centuries of papal supremacy, foretold in Daniel 7:25 and Revelation 12:6. All these tribulations occurred under either pagan or papal Rome.

For whose sake would the period be shortened?

"And except those days should be shortened, there should no flesh be saved: but *for the elect's sake those days shall be shortened."* Verse 22.

NOTE.—Through the influence of the Reformation of the sixteenth century, and the movements which grew out of it, the power of the papacy to enforce its decrees against those it pronounced heretics was gradually lessened, until general persecution ceased almost wholly by the middle of the eighteenth century, before the 1260 years ended.

Against what deceptions did Christ then warn us?

"Then if any man shall say unto you, Lo, here is Christ, or there; believe it not. For there shall arise false Christs, and false prophets, and shall shew great signs and wonders; insomuch that, if it were possible, they shall deceive the very elect." Verses 23, 24.

What signs of the end would be seen in the heavens?

"There shall be signs in the *sun,* and in the *moon,* and in the *stars."* Luke 21:25.

When were the first of these signs to appear?

"Immediately after the tribulation of those days shall the sun be darkened, and the moon shall not give her light, and the stars shall fall from heaven." Matthew 24:29.

"But *in those days, after that tribulation,* the sun shall

be darkened, and the moon shall not give her light, and the stars of heaven shall fall, and the powers that are in heaven shall be shaken." Mark 13:24, 25. Compare Joel 2:30, 31; 3:15; Isaiah 13:10; Amos 8:9.

NOTE.—Within the 1260 years, but after the persecution (about the middle of the eighteenth century), the signs of His coming began to appear.

1. *A wonderful darkening of the sun and moon.* The remarkable dark day of May 19, 1780, is described by Samuel Williams of Harvard. The professor relates that the obscuration approached with the clouds from the southwest "between the hours of ten and eleven A.M. and continued until the middle of the next night," varying in degree and duration in different localities. In some places "persons could not see to read common print in the open air, for several hours," although "this was not generally the case." "Candles were lighted up in the houses;—the birds having sung their evening songs, disappeared, and became silent;—the fowls retired to roost;—the cocks were crowing all around, as at break of day;—objects could not be distinguished but at a very little distance; and everything bore the appearance and gloom of night." (See *Memoirs of the American Academy of Arts and Sciences* [through 1783], vol. 1, pp, 234, 235.)

Since the moon, full the night before, was on the opposite side of the earth, there was no eclipse of the sun—nor could an eclipse last so long. The causes assigned seem inadequate to account for the area covered.

"The darkness of *the following evening* was probably as gross as ever has been observed since the Almighty fiat gave birth to light. It wanted only palpability to render it as extraordinary, as that which overspread the land of Egypt in the days of Moses. . . . If every luminous body in the universe had been shrouded in impenetrable shades, or struck out of existence, the darkness could not have been more complete. A sheet of white paper held within a few inches of the eyes was equally invisible with the blackest velvet."—SAMUEL TENNEY, Letter (1785) in *Collections of the Massachusetts Historical Society,* part 1, vol. 1 (1792 ed.), pp. 97, 98.

Timothy Dwight, president of Yale, remembered that "a very general opinion prevailed, that the day of judgment was at hand. The [Connecticut] House of Representatives, being unable to transact their business, adjourned," but the Council lighted candles, preferring, as a member said, to be found at work if the judgment were approaching. (See John W. Barber, *Connecticut Historical Collections* [2d ed., 1836], p. 403.)

There was no agreement among the current writers as to the cause of this unparalleled darkness, but there was entire agreement as to the extraordinary character of it. Any suggestion of a natural cause or causes for the darkness can in no wise militate against the significance of the event. Sixteen and a half centuries before it occurred the Saviour had definitely foretold this twofold sign, saying, "In those days after that tribulation, the sun shall be darkened, and the moon shall not give her light." Mark 13:24. These signs occurred exactly as predicted, and at the time indicated so long before their occurrence. It is this fact, and not the cause of the darkness, that is significant in this connection. When the Lord would open a path for His people through the sea, He did it by "a strong east wind." Exodus 14:21. Was it for this reason any less miraculous? When the bitter waters were made sweet (Exodus 15:23-25), was the divine interposition any less real because certain natural means were used, having apparently some part, under divine direction, in rendering the water fit for drinking? In like manner, even though it were possible for science to account for the remarkable darkness of May 19, 1780, instead of merely speculating concerning it, the event would not be discredited thereby as a merciful sign of the approaching end of probationary time.

2. *Remarkable display of falling stars.*

"The morning of November 13th, 1833," says an eyewitness, a Yale astronomer, "was rendered memorable by an exhibition of the phenomenon called shooting stars, which was probably more extensive and magnificent than any similar one hitherto recorded. . . . Probably no celestial phenomenon has ever occurred in this country, since its first settlement, which was viewed with so much admiration and delight by one class of spectators, or with so much astonishment and fear by another class."—DENISON OLMSTED in *The American Journal of Science and Arts*, vol. 25 (1834), pp. 363, 364.

"From the Gulf of Mexico to Halifax, until daylight with some difficulty put an end to the display, the sky was scored in every direction with shining tracks and illuminated with majestic fireballs. At Boston, the frequency of meteors was estimated to be about half that of flakes of snow in an average snowstorm. . . . Traced backwards, their paths were invariably found to converge to a point in the constellation Leo."—AGNES M. CLERKE, *A Popular History of Astronomy* (1885 ed.), pp. 369, 370.

What were to be the signs on earth of Christ's coming?

"Distress of nations, with perplexity; *the sea and the waves roaring; men's hearts failing them for fear,* and for looking after those things which are coming on the earth." Luke 21:25, 26.

What was to be the next great event after these signs?

"And then shall they see *the Son of man coming in a cloud with power and great glory."* Verse 27. (See Matthew 24:30.)

When these things *begin* to happen, what should we do?

"And when these things begin to come to pass, then *look up, and lift up your heads;* for your redemption draweth nigh." Luke 21:28.

When the trees put forth their leaves, what do we know?

"Now learn a parable of the fig tree; When his branch is yet tender, and putteth forth leaves, *ye know that summer is nigh."* Matthew 24:32.

What do we likewise know after these signs are seen?

"So likewise ye, when ye shall see all these things, *know that it is near, even at the doors."* Verse 33. "So likewise ye, when ye see these things come to pass, *know ye that the kingdom of God is nigh at hand."* Luke 21:31.

What did Christ say of the certainty of this prophecy?

"Verily I say unto you, This generation shall not pass, till all these things be fulfilled. Heaven and earth shall pass away, but my words shall not pass away." Matthew 24:34, 35.

NOTE.—What Christ foretold of the destruction of Jerusalem came true to the very letter. Likewise may we be assured that what He has said about the end of the world will as certainly and as literally be fulfilled.

Who alone knows the exact day of Christ's coming?

"But of that day and hour *knoweth no man,* no, not the angels of heaven, but *my Father only."* Verse 36.

What moral conditions would precede Christ's second advent?

"But as the days of Noe were, so shall also the coming of the Son of man be. For as in the days that were before the flood they were *eating* and *drinking, marrying* and *giving in marriage,* until the day that Noe entered into the ark, and knew not until the flood came, and took them all away; *so shall also the coming of the Son of man be."* Verses 37-39.

What important admonition has Christ given us?

"Therefore *be ye also ready:* for in such an hour as ye think not the Son of man cometh." Verse 44.

What will be the experience of those who say in their hearts that the Lord is not soon coming?

"If that evil servant shall say in his heart, My lord delayeth his coming; and shall begin to smite his fellow-servants, and to eat and drink with the drunken; the lord of that servant shall come in a day when he looketh not for him, and in an hour that he is not aware of, and shall cut him asunder ["cut him off," margin], and appoint him his portion with the hypocrites: there shall be weeping and gnashing of teeth." Verses 48-51.

Christ's
Second Coming

What promise did Christ make concerning His coming?

"Let not your heart be troubled: ye believe in God, believe also in me. In my Father's house are many mansions: if it were not so, I would have told you. I go to prepare a place for you. And if I go and prepare a place for you, *I will come again,* and receive you unto myself; that where I am, there ye may be also." John 14:1-3.

What follows the signs of Christ's coming?

"And then shall they see *the Son of man coming in a cloud with power and great glory.*" Luke 21:27.

At His ascension, how was Christ's return promised?

"And while they looked stedfastly toward heaven as he went up, behold, two men stood by them in white apparel; which also said, Ye men of Galilee, why stand ye gazing up into heaven? *this same Jesus, which is taken up from you into heaven, shall so come in like manner as ye have seen him go into heaven.*" Acts 1:10, 11.

How does Paul give expression to this hope?

"Looking for that blessed hope, and the glorious appearing of the great God and our Saviour Jesus Christ." Titus 2:13.

What is Peter's testimony regarding it?

"We have not followed cunningly devised fables, when we made known unto you the power and coming of our Lord Jesus Christ, but were eyewitnesses of his majesty." 2 Peter 1:16.

Will the inhabitants of the earth as a whole be prepared to meet Him?

"Then shall appear the sign of the Son of man in heaven: and *then shall all the tribes of the earth mourn,* and they shall see the Son of man coming in the clouds of heaven with power and great glory." Matthew 24:30. "Behold, he cometh with clouds; and every eye shall see him, and they also which pierced him: and *all kindreds of the earth shall wail because of him."* Revelation 1:7.

Why will many not be prepared for this event?

"But and if that evil servant shall say in his heart, *My lord delayeth his coming;* and shall begin to smite his fellowservants, and to eat and drink with the drunken; the lord of that servant shall come in a day when he looketh not for him, and in an hour that he is not aware of, and shall cut him asunder, and appoint him his portion with the hypocrites: there shall be weeping and gnashing of teeth." Matthew 24:48-51.

What will the world be doing when Christ comes?

"But as the days of Noe were, so shall also the coming of the Son of man be. For as in the days that were before the flood *they were eating and drinking, marrying and giving in marriage,* until the day that Noe entered into the ark, and knew not until the flood came, and took them all away; so shall also the coming of the Son of man be." Verses 37-39. "Likewise also as it was in the days of Lot; *they did eat, they drank, they bought, they sold, they planted, they builded;* but the same day that Lot went out of Sodom it rained fire and brimstone from heaven, and destroyed them all. Even thus shall it be in the day when the Son of man is revealed." Luke 17:28-30.

NOTE.—These texts do not teach that it is wrong in itself to eat, drink, marry, buy, sell, plant, or build, but that men's minds will be so taken up with these things that they will give little or no thought to the future life, and make no plans or preparation to meet Jesus when He comes.

Who is it that blinds men to the gospel of Christ?

"In whom *the god of this world* [Satan] hath blinded the minds of them which believe not, lest the light of the glorious gospel of Christ, who is the image of God, should shine unto them." 2 Corinthians 4:4.

NOTE.—"To my mind this precious doctrine—for such I must call it—of the return of the Lord to this earth is taught in the New Testament as clearly as any other doctrine in it; yet I was in the Church fifteen or sixteen years before I ever heard a sermon on it. There is hardly any church that doesn't make a great deal of baptism, but in all of Paul's epistles I believe baptism is only spoken of thirteen times, while it speaks about the return of our Lord fifty times; and yet the Church has had very little to say about it. Now, I can see a reason for this; the devil does not want us to see this truth, for nothing would wake up the Church so much. The moment a man takes hold of the truth that Jesus Christ is coming again to receive His followers to Himself, this world loses its hold upon him. Gas stocks and water stocks and stocks in banks and railroads are of very much less consequence to him then. His heart is free, and he looks for the blessed appearing of his Lord, who, at His coming, will take him into His blessed Kingdom."—D. L. MOODY, *The Second Coming of Christ* (Revell), pp. 6, 7.

"'This same Jesus, which is taken up from you into heaven, *shall so come in like manner as ye have seen him go into heaven,*' is the parting promise of Jesus to his disciples, communicated through the two men in white apparel, as a cloud received him out of their sight. When after more than fifty years in glory he breaks the silence and speaks once more in the Revelation which he gave to his servant John, the post-ascension Gospel which he sends opens with, '*Be-*

hold, He cometh with clouds,' and closes with *'Surely I come quickly.'* Considering the solemn emphasis thus laid upon this doctrine, and considering the great prominence given to it throughout the teaching of our Lord and of his apostles, how was it that for the first five years of my pastoral life it had absolutely no place in my preaching? Undoubtedly the reason lay in the lack of early instruction. Of all the sermons heard from childhood on, I do not remember listening to a single one upon this subject."—A. J. GORDON, *How Christ Came to Church,* pp. 44, 45.

When are the saved to be like Jesus?

"Beloved, now are we the sons of God, and it doth not yet appear what we shall be: but we know that, *when he shall appear, we shall be like him;* for we shall see him as he is." 1 John 3:2.

Will Christ's coming be a time of reward?

"For the Son of man shall come in the glory of his Father with his angels; and *then he shall reward every man according to his works.*" Matthew 16:27. "And, behold, I come quickly; *and my reward is with me,* to give every man according as his work shall be." Revelation 22:12.

To whom is salvation promised at Christ's appearing?

"So Christ was once offered to bear the sins of many; and *unto them that look for him* shall he appear the second time without sin unto salvation." Hebrews 9:28.

What influence has this hope upon the life?

"We know that, when he shall appear, we shall be like him; for we shall see him as he is. And *every man that hath this hope in him purifieth himself, even as he is pure.*" 1 John 3:2, 3.

To whom is a crown of righteousness promised?

"For I am now ready to be offered, and the time of my departure is at hand. I have fought a good fight, I have finished my course, I have kept the faith: henceforth there is laid up for me a crown of righteousness, which the Lord, the righteous judge, shall give me at that day: and not to me only, but *unto all them also that love his appearing.*" 2 Timothy 4:6-8.

What will the waiting ones say when Jesus comes?

"And it shall be said in that day, Lo, this is our God; we have waited for him, and he will save us: this is the Lord; we have waited for him, we will be glad and rejoice in his salvation." Isaiah 25:9.

Has the exact time of Christ's coming been revealed?

"But of that day and hour *knoweth no man,* no, not the angels of heaven, but my Father only." Matthew 24:36.

In view of this fact, what does Christ tell us to do?

"Watch therefore: for ye know not what hour your Lord doth come." Verse 42.

NOTE.—"To the secure and careless He will come as a thief in the night: to His own, as their Lord."—HENRY ALFORD, *The New Testament for English Readers,* vol. 1, part 1, p. 170.

"The proper attitude of a Christian is to be always looking for his Lord's return."—D. L. MOODY, *The Second Coming of Christ* (Revell), p. 9.

What warning has Christ given that we might not be taken by surprise by this great event?

"And take heed to yourselves, lest at any time your hearts be overcharged with surfeiting, and drunkenness, and cares of this life, and so that day come upon you unawares. For as a snare shall it come on all them that dwell on the face of the whole earth. Watch ye therefore, and pray always, that ye may be accounted worthy to escape all these things that shall come to pass, and to stand before the Son of man." Luke 21:34-36.

What Christian grace are we exhorted to exercise in our expectant longing for this event?

"Be *patient* therefore, brethren, unto the coming of the Lord. Behold, the husbandman waiteth for the precious fruit of the earth, and hath long patience for it, until he receive the early and latter rain. Be ye also *patient;* stablish your hearts: for the coming of the Lord draweth nigh." James 5:7, 8.

The Home
of the Saved

For what purpose was the earth created?

"For thus saith the Lord that created the heavens; God himself that formed the earth and made it; he hath established it, he created it not in vain, *he formed it to be inhabited.*" Isaiah 45:18.

To whom has God given the earth?

"The heaven, even the heavens, are the Lord's: but *the earth hath he given to the children of men.*" Psalm 115:16.

For what purpose was man made?

"Thou madest him *to have dominion over the works of thy hands;* thou hast put all things under his feet." Psalm 8:6.

How did man lose his dominion?

Through sin. Romans 5:12; 6:23.

When man lost his dominion, to whom did he yield it?

"For of whom a man is overcome, of the same is he brought in bondage." 2 Peter 2:19.

NOTE.—Man was overcome by Satan in the Garden of Eden, and there yielded himself and his possessions into the hands of his captor.

In tempting Christ, what ownership did Satan claim?

"And the devil, taking him up into an high mountain, shewed unto him all the kingdoms of the world in a moment of time. And the devil said unto him, All this power will I give thee, and the glory of them: *for that is delivered unto me; and to whomsoever I will I give it."* Luke 4:5, 6.

What promise of restoration did the Lord make through Micah?

"And thou, *O tower of the flock,* the strong hold of the daughter of Zion, *unto thee shall it come, even the first dominion;* the kingdom shall come to the daughter of Jerusalem." Micah 4:8.

Why did Christ say the meek are blessed?

"Blessed are the meek: *for they shall inherit the earth."* Matthew 5:5.

NOTE.—This inheritance cannot be realized in this life, for here the truly meek generally have little of earth's good things.

Who does the psalmist say have most now?

"For I was envious at *the foolish,* when I saw the prosperity of *the wicked.* . . . Their eyes stand out with fatness: *they have more than heart could wish."* Psalm 73:3-7.

What promise was made to Abraham concerning the land?

"And the Lord said unto Abram, after that Lot was separated from him, Lift up now thine eyes, and look from the place where thou art northward, and southward, and eastward, and westward: for *all the land which thou seest, to thee will I give it, and to thy* SEED *for ever."* Genesis 13:14, 15.

How much did this promise comprehend?

"For the promise, that he should be the heir of the world, was not to Abraham, or to his seed, through the law, but through the righteousness of faith." Romans 4:13.

How much of the land of Canaan did Abraham own in his lifetime?

"And he gave him none inheritance in it, no, not so much as to set his foot on: yet he promised that he would give it to him for a possession, and to his seed after him, when as yet he had no child." Acts 7:5. (See Hebrews 11:13.)

In a special sense, who is the seed to whom this promise was made?

"Now to Abraham and his seed were the promises made. He saith not, And to seeds, as of many; but as of one, *And to thy seed, which is Christ."* Galatians 3:16.

Who are heirs of the promise?

"And *if ye be Christ's, then are ye Abraham's seed, and heirs according to the promise."* Verse 29.

Why did not these ancient worthies receive the promise?

"And these all, having obtained a good report through faith, received not the promise: God having provided some better thing for us, *that they without us should not be made perfect."* Hebrews 11:39, 40.

What is to become of our earth in the day of the Lord?

"But the day of the Lord will come as a thief in the night; in the which the heavens shall pass away with a great noise, and *the elements shall melt with fervent heat, the earth also and the works that are therein shall be burned up."* 2 Peter 3:10.

What will follow this great conflagration?

"Nevertheless we, according to his promise, *look for new heavens and a new earth,* wherein dwelleth righteousness." Verse 13.

NOTE.—At the coming of Christ the living wicked will die, and the saints will be taken to heaven to dwell with Christ a thousand years, or until the wicked of all ages are judged and the time comes for their destruction and the purification of the earth by the fires of the last day. Following this, the earth will be formed anew, and man, redeemed from sin, will be restored to his original dominion.

To what Old Testament promise did Peter evidently refer?

"For, behold, I create new heavens and a new earth: and the former shall not be remembered, nor come into mind." Isaiah 65:17.

What was shown the apostle John in vision?

"And I saw *a new heaven and a new earth:* for the first heaven and the first earth were passed away; and there was no more sea." Revelation 21:1.

How did Isaiah describe conditions on the "new earth"?

"And they shall build houses, and inhabit them; and they shall plant vineyards, and eat the fruit of them. They shall not build and another inhabit; they shall not plant, and another eat: for as the days of a tree are the days of my people, and mine elect shall long enjoy the work of their hands. They shall not labour in vain, nor bring forth for trouble; for they are the seed of the blessed of the Lord, and their offspring with them." Isaiah 65:21-23.

How readily will their wants be supplied?

"And it shall come to pass, that before they call, I will answer; and while they are yet speaking, I will hear." Verse 24.

What peaceful condition will reign throughout the earth then?

"The wolf and the lamb shall feed together, and the lion shall eat straw like the bullock: and dust shall be the serpent's meat. They shall not hurt nor destroy in all my holy mountain, saith the Lord." Verse 25.

What seasons of worship will be observed in the new earth?

"For as the new heavens and the new earth, which I will make, shall remain before me, saith the Lord, so shall your seed and your name remain. And it shall come to pass, that *from one new moon to another, and from one sabbath to another,* shall all flesh come to worship before me, saith the Lord." Isaiah 66:22, 23.

What will the ransomed of the Lord then do?

"*And the ransomed of the Lord shall return, and come to Zion with songs and everlasting joy upon their heads:* they shall obtain joy and gladness, and sorrow and sighing shall flee away." Isaiah 35:10.

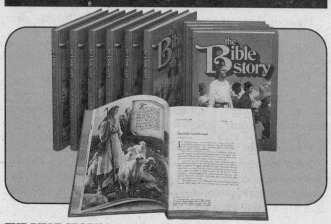

BOOKS TO ENRICH YOUR LIFE

The Desire of Ages

This is E. G. White's classic best-seller on the life of Christ. It is perhaps the most beautiful of the Saviour's biographies since Matthew, Mark, Luke, and John. New hope and courage will fill your heart when you see Jesus as the merciful Redeemer of sinners; as the Healer of human ills; as the tender, compassionate Friend; and as the coming King. Includes 65 full-page color paintings.

The Triumph of God's Love

The Bible tells of a continuing conflict between God's people and the forces of evil. But what has happened in that war since Bible times? This two-volume set shows the embattled history of the Christian church after the last chapter of Revelation. It even looks ahead to the final victory at the end of time.

Bible Readings for the Home

Here's an easy way to find Bible answers to your questions. This-two volume set organizes 4,000 questions so that you can quickly refer to the ones that concern you most. And the answer you read comes straight from the Bible. No modern sermonizing. Just the plain words of a Bible text.

The Bible Reference Library

(pictured) includes the above three titles and offers a complete, easy-to-understand Bible commentary for adults.

NOTES

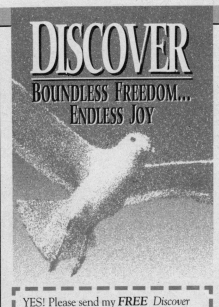

NOTES